Mastering the Mound

A Pitcher's Guide to Dominance

From the Stretch

The Art and Science of Pitching

Sky Benson

Table of Contents

CHAPTER 1

THE PITCHER'S TOOLBOX

Breaking down

"The different types of pitches"

Picture yourself on the mound, staring down the batter with a lot of stress in the air. What do you do? A small white sphere is used to trick and beat them. How, though? That's where the arsenal of pitches comes in. Each one has its attitude and goal.

The Fastball: Who's in Charge?

You could say that the fastball is the king of pitches. The white blur that screams at the batter is the rocket on fire. That pitch gets everyone excited—the one that hits hard and fast. Two types of fastballs are the four-seam fastball, which goes straight, and the two-seam fastball, which sinks and rides down like a roller coaster, making it harder to hit the ball.

Benders and Dippers are part of the Breaking Ball Brigade.

Let's move on to the breaking balls. These pitches, like magicians, move in strange ways that seem to fight gravity. The curveball falls sharply like a star and is the traditional breaker. The slider is the other pitch. Its path sharpens to the side, leaving the hitter to swing at nothing. Some people even throw a slurve, a mix of the two, moving both down and sideways. Furthermore, there is the screwball, a pitch that wobbles in a way that is hard to predict and can confuse even the most experienced pitchers.

The Switch up: How to Lie Your Way Around

Picture throwing a fastball, and suddenly, it slows down like a car putting on the brakes. That's what the changeup does. This pitch is meant to surprise the hitter, which throws off their timing and often leads to weak contact, a swing, and a miss. It's sneaky, like a ninja, and the player is caught off guard by the sudden change in speed.

Beyond the Basics: Adding to the Guns

Some pitchers, the real experts in their field, throw pitches that aren't on the list. For example, the splitter is a fastball with a quick drop to the ground, making its path resemble a split. They also have the cutter, a fastball that moves quickly from side to side. For those who want something truly special, there is the forkball, a slow pitch with a late, dramatic drop that can fool even the most experienced batters.

It takes a lifetime to get good at these throws. It takes a lot of practice to get good at it, work on your grip, and understand each ball's subtleties. You'll be a pitcher with many tricks when you do, ready to trick and beat any hitter who comes up to bat.

The mechanics of pitching

Picture yourself standing on the field and hearing the crowd roaring far away. As each second goes by, the stress grows as the batter stares you down. Then, in a rush of motion, you let out a pitch that doesn't make sense. But how does hitting a baseball, which looks like it would be easy, lead to pinpoint accuracy and devastating speed? It all comes down to the complicated dance of how pitches work.

Where it all began: the grip

The grip is the most essential part of your throwing arsenal. How you hold the ball affects the pitch you throw and how it moves inside the field. Each pitch has its grip, and the best results come from placing your fingers in specific ways and applying the right amount of pressure. For example, a four-seam grip might be needed for a fastball to go straight, while a certain amount of sideways pressure is required for a curveball to break down.

The Big Unfolding: The Giving

Now, think of the pitching motion as an orchestra that works well together. Like a coiled spring, your body prepares to start in the windup or stretch pose. The next move is the leg drive, your strong push off the pitch that sends force up. This energy goes through your core and into your arm swing, which ends with you letting go of the ball. Every step in this process must go smoothly and quickly so that the results are accurate and the risk of hurt is low.

The Important Moment: The Let Go Point

Think of the release point as the pitching symphony's director. It's when the ball leaves your hand, greatly affecting how the pitch moves and where it goes. A consistent release point is crucial for control because it ensures the ball goes in a known direction toward the batter. It's like aiming a laser pointer—any small change can throw you off goal.

The Core and Lower Body Are the Powerhouse

If you want to pitch, you must use your whole body, not just your arm. A strong core and lower body are like a power plant; they make the force that turns into speed. Think of your core as a stable base that moves the energy from your legs to your arms. Strong legs give the initial push that moves you forward and gives your arm swing force.

Repeating and improving things is the key to being consistent.

Mastering the basics of pitching is a process, not a goal. It takes a tremendous amount of time to practice, repeat, and get better at it. Heavy balls and long throws are drills that help build arm strength and accuracy. You can find places to improve your skills by watching video recordings of them. Always remember that it's like learning a language: the more you do it, the better you get at it.

The Pros: Accuracy, Speed, and Avoiding Injuries

It's not enough to throw hard; good techniques are essential for accuracy and control. If you can throw the ball well, it will go where you want it to, making it very hard for batters to hit. Also, good mechanics keep your arm from being stressed, which lowers the risk of damage and lets you pitch for years to come. Now, the next time you see a pitcher throw a fastball or a curveball, keep these complicated movements in mind. Years of hard work, much practice, and a deep knowledge of how to throw a baseball are all shown by that.

Why the Pitcher's Engine Works: Building Endurance and Arm Strength

Think of a car engine roaring with power and moving the car forward effortlessly. That's what arm strength and stamina are all about for a pitcher. It means throwing pitch after pitch with the same speed and accuracy, which keeps batters wondering and the game under control. But how do you make this engine?

The Base: A Well-Designed Throwing Program

A throwing program is like a well-thought-out road map. It slowly makes your arm stronger and more durable, which keeps you from getting overuse injuries and sets you up for long-term success. This program includes several different parts:

Long Toss: To do this exercise, throw the ball as far as possible, which helps build arm strength by imitating the throwing motion.

Like stretching a rubber band, the more you do it, the stronger it gets.

Weighted Balls: Using balls heavier than a baseball increases resistance, making your muscles work harder and adapt. For example, when you lift weights, the more weight you put on, the stronger your muscles get.

Drills: Different muscle groups used in throwing are worked on by different drills, such as core strengthening, scapular stabilization, and external and internal movements. Imagine working on other engine parts to ensure they work at their best.

More Than the Basics: Recovery and Conditioning

It's not enough to just be able to throw things; you need to build a strong base all around. A strong core keeps you stable and moves power from your legs to your arms quickly and effectively. Strong legs give you the initial push that moves your body forward and gives your arm swing force. It's like a strong frame holding up the powerful engine.

Recovery is just as important: Getting enough rest lets your muscles heal and grow back, which keeps you from getting tired or hurt. Getting enough sleep is very important, and active healing methods like foam rolling, stretching, and massage help you get better faster and keep your performance at its best. Imagine giving your engine regular care to ensure it keeps running well for years.

The Journey: Being Patient and Committed

Not a sprint, but a run to get more muscular arms and faster. You have to be patient and dedicated and follow a planned program. Keep things the same, even when the season is over. Don't forget that success takes time and that pushing too hard can make things worse. Pay attention to your body, take days off when needed, and slowly build up the time and effort you put into your workouts.

Control, power, and long life are the rewards.

Having a strong arm and a lot of stamina is good for you. Because you'll have more control over your pitches, you can paint the strike zone and throw batters off balance. You become a stronger pitcher on the field when your velocity increases because it leads to more strikeouts and weaker contact. The most important thing is that good training and conditioning lower the risk of injury. This means you can pitch for years and enjoy the long and gratifying journey of being a pitcher. This means that the next time you see a pitcher throw a hard-hitting fastball or a tricky curveball, think about all the time and effort that went into making those throws possible. It shows how hard they've worked to make their bodywork like a machine that can win games from the pitch.

Building endurance

"And arm strength"

Imagine a pitcher is on the mound, and they are releasing a fastball that is blistering or a deceptive curveball. A considerable amount of strength and endurance lurks behind that throw that appears effortless. To construct this foundation, it is not enough to throw more forcefully; instead, it is necessary to build an engine capable of withstanding the demands of the game, pitch after pitch. To become a pitcher capable of dominating the game, what are the steps to building this engine?

A structured throwing program is outlined in the road map.

Imagine a throwing program as a meticulously planned road map that leads to the highest possible level of performance. It is a scheduled routine that will gradually enhance your arm strength and endurance, reducing problems caused by overuse and laying the groundwork for success in the long run. The longer you stretch it, the more powerful it becomes. This is how the long toss works. Long toss exercises can increase arm strength and endurance by gradually increasing the thrown distance. These exercises are designed to simulate the motion of throwing. It would be best to begin with small throws and progressively increase the distance as your arm becomes more accustomed to the move. The bigger the load, the stronger your muscles get. This is the same principle that applies to weighted balls. Adding weighted balls to your throwing action provides resistance, forcing your muscles to work harder and adapt to the new demands. To enhance your strength, you should begin with lesser weights and progressively raise the weight as you progress. A good analogy for drills is working on various components of an automobile engine to get maximum performance. External and internal rotations, scapular stabilization exercises, and core strengthening exercises are specific drills that target different muscle groups involved in throwing. It is possible to prevent muscular imbalances that might lead to injuries by performing these workouts, which assist in building balanced strength.

Getting Beyond the Fundamentals: Conditioning and Recuperation

It is not enough to throw to increase arm strength; it is necessary to construct a solid foundation. Imagine that a well-built chassis supports a powerful engine. With a strong core, you can maintain balance and effectively transfer power from your legs to your arms. Your legs should be strong since they are responsible for the first push, which propels your body forward and creates momentum for the arm swing. To construct a solid foundation for throwing action, you must incorporate workouts that strengthen your core and legs into your personal training program. In the same vein, recovery is essential. Imagine maintaining your engine regularly to continue functioning without problems for many years. Your muscles can repair and renew themselves when you get enough rest, which helps prevent weariness and injury. Active recovery techniques such as stretching, massage, and foam rolling encourage speedier recovery and sustain peak performance. Proper sleep is crucial; these practices are key to maintaining peak performance. If you want to avoid experiencing setbacks, it is important to pay attention to your body, take rest days when they are required, and avoid pushing yourself too hard.

Overcoming Obstacles Through Patience and Dedication

Strength and endurance training for the arms is more of a marathon than a sprint. Patience, persistence, and a commitment to following a disciplined program are all necessary. Even during the offseason, consistency is of the utmost importance. Remember that making progress takes time, and exerting too much effort can result in injuries. Pay attention to what your body is telling you, take days off when necessary, and take baby steps to improve the intensity and duration of your workouts.

Control, power, and longevity are the benefits it offers

There is no denying the advantages of having a strong arm and decent endurance. Just picture yourself painting the edges of the strike zone with pinpoint accuracy, using a variety of pitches to throw batters off balance and keep them off balance. Increasing your velocity can strike out more batters and make less contact with the ball, making you a more dominant force on the mound. Not only does excellent training and conditioning reduce the likelihood of injury, but it also enables you to continue pitching for many years, allowing you to take pleasure in the lengthy and satisfying journey of being a pitcher. When you next witness a pitcher release a blistering fastball or a sneaky curveball, it is important to remember the commitment and effort that went into establishing the engine behind those throws. Their dedication to transforming their body into a well-oiled machine that is capable of dominating the game from the mound is demonstrated by this particular accomplishment.

CHAPTER 2

COMMANDING THE STRIKE ZONE

Strategies for pitch control

Imagine you are standing on the mound, and the crowd's roar is a faint murmur in the distance. The ball is in your grasp, and you are prepared to unleash your arsenal of pitches. However, the secret to success is not simply throwing hard but striking with precise accuracy. To become an expert in the art of pitch control, here are several strategies:

Putting Together a Strong Base: The Importance of Mechanics

Take, for example, a house; the foundation is extremely important to the house's overall stability. Similarly, the foundation of pitch control is ensuring that pitching mechanics are consistent.

Grip: The movement of each pitch is determined by a certain grip at that particular pitch. To throw accurately, it is essential to master these grips and maintain consistent finger placement continually. Modifying the grip even slightly can significantly impact the trajectory of the ball.

The pitching motion should be pictured as a well-coordinated ballet for delivery. Smoothness and efficiency are required in every phase, beginning with the windup or stretch and continuing through the leg drive and arm swing. The mechanics are inconsistent, which results in the ball moving in unanticipated ways and missing areas. The release point is analogous to aiming a laser pointer; even the slightest deviation causes the target to be thrown off. The point at which the ball is released, or the precise instant it leaves your hand, considerably impacts its trajectory. A consistent release point ensures the ball will move in your intended direction.

The Strike Zone: A Strategic Game of Targeting the Strike Zone

Imagine that the strike zone is a painting and that you are the artist holding the paintbrush (or, in this case, the baseball). To achieve mastery of pitch control, it is necessary to strategically position the ball within this zone to keep the batter guessing. You should develop your aim points to improve your ability to throw to particular spots within the striking zone. It is necessary to grasp the various aiming spots and adjust to the batter's stance and tendencies to accomplish this. It is possible, for instance, that a righthanded batter would benefit from receiving a fastball that is thrown high and inside. When it comes to sequencing, throwing pitches in an intelligent order is essential. When fastballs and off-speed pitches are combined, the batter's timing is thrown off, making it more difficult to anticipate what will happen next. A changeup thrown after a fastball can make the fastball appear much slower, throwing the batter off balance.

Hitters: The Art of Deception is a book that reading

Consider a game of chess in which you try to guess your opponent's moves. Reading hitters is comparable to this. You can analyze their tendencies through scouting reports or observation while playing to take advantage of their flaws. Batters frequently display subtle body language clues that reflect their anticipation of certain pitches. Recognizing these tells is essential. A hitter can adjust their stance slightly or improve their grip on the bat in response to what they anticipate. It would help if you learned to interpret these tells to get an advantage and throw pitches they do not expect. The game is a dynamic environment requiring players to adapt in real-time. You should always be ready to modify your pitching strategy in response to the batter's performance as well as the circumstances of the game. If you want to vary the game's pace, consider throwing a curveball to a batter who keeps fouling off fastballs.

A Concentration of the Mind: The Power of the Mind

Consider a laser beam: even a tiny shake in your hand can cause it to divert from its intended path. Likewise, mental concentration is an essential component of pitch control. Before you get onto the mound, give yourself a mental image of yourself pitching strikes with pinpoint accuracy. Through mental rehearsal, one can increase self-assurance and strengthen the mechanics necessary for accuracy.

Maintaining Your Calm: Although pressure is unavoidable, you should not let it influence your mechanics. Take a few slow, deep breaths, concentrate on your objective, and have faith in training. Being shaken up can cause one to throw erratically and miss spots on the target. Recurring errors from the past should not be a source of distraction. With each new pitch comes a fresh opportunity. Learn from your mistakes, adjust your strategy, and concentrate on the next toss you make.

The Path to Mastery: The Proverb "Practice Makes Perfect"

It is important to remember that learning pitch control is a process, not a destination. It requires a significant amount of practice, the refinement of technique, and an awareness of the subtleties present in each pitch. Practice drills that emphasize precision regularly, such as throwing to specified targets or mimicking game circumstances. Repetition drills are a great way to improve your accuracy. Through repetition, good mechanics can be strengthened, and muscle memory can be developed.

Input and Adjustments: Getting feedback from your coaches or teammates regarding your mechanics and release point is important. It would be best to examine the video recordings to locate areas that could be improved and then make any necessary improvements.

By putting these tactics into action and devoting yourself to persistent practice, you may turn yourself from a wild thrower into a master of pitch control. This will allow you to become a pitcher who consistently paints the corners of the strike zone and controls the game.

Reading hitters

"And exploiting weaknesses."

Assume that you are on the mound and that you are engaged in a contest of wits with the hitter who is located across the diamond. Not only is it important to throw forcefully, but it is also important to outsmart your opponent, anticipate their moves, and take advantage of their weaknesses. This is where the skill of reading hitters comes into play; it is a skill that differentiates pitchers who are good from those who are amazing.

Conducting Scouting and Observation to Become a Hitter Whisperer

Imagine a detective carefully collecting clues to solve a case. You should know about the batter you will face before you get onto the mound. The reports from the scouting program offer vital insights into their:

Righthanded batters: Those standing near the plate may be more sensitive to inside pitches, whereas righthanded batters with a wider stance may imply that they favor pitches that are further away from the plate.

Swing mechanics: Does the batter have a compact, flat swing or a long, looping swing? What is the difference between the two? The types of pitches most likely to be successful can be impacted. Does the batter have a history of chasing breaking balls or laboring against fastballs high in the zone? This is referred to as the batter's pitching tendencies. It is possible that recognizing these characteristics will provide you with a substantial edge. Studying the batter during warmups and their previous at-bats is important. Take note of:

- **Body Language:** Subtle variations in weight distribution or hand position may give a tell about the individual's anticipation of particular pitches.

- **Bat Grip:** A closed stance with the hands close together may show that the batter is concentrating on inside pitches, whereas a wider grip may suggest that the batter is anticipating something to come from the other direction.

The Art of Deception: Providing Something That They Are Not Anticipating

Think of a magician plucking a rabbit out of a hat. Just imagine it. When it comes to taking advantage of a hitter's deficiencies, the element of surprise is essential. Don't be predictable when it comes to sequencing. Changing the game's pace and keeping the batter off balance can be accomplished by combining fastballs and off-speed deliveries. To make a fastball appear considerably slower, throw a changeup after it or surprise them with a curveball following a streak of fastballs. Both of these strategies are effective. It would help if you made proposals to exploit their vulnerabilities based on your location observations. It would be best if you threw a high and tight fastball for a batter with trouble with inside pitches. On the other hand, a curveball that is down in the zone should be thrown to a batter pursuing breaking balls.

Adapting in Real-time: The Game That Is Always Growing

Imagine playing a game of chess in which you are continually adjusting your strategy in response to the moves made by your opponent. Batters can make modifications throughout their at-bat because hitting is a dynamic process that is constantly changing. When a batter begins to lay off breaking balls, you should throw more fastballs. This is an example of recognizing adjustments. Mix in more pitches slower than the fastball if they appear to anticipate the fastball. If you want to notice changes in their approach, pay close attention to their body language and swing mechanics. Putting Your Faith in Your Instincts. Even after all of the planning and preparation, there are moments when your instincts can be the most reliable guide. If you feel a particular pitch is the best option, you should obey your gut feelings and carry out the pitch with self-assurance.

Keeping one step ahead of the competition is the power of mental focus.

Like a laser beam, even a tiny shake in your hand might cause it to divert from its intended path. Similarly, mental concentration is an essential component in the process of reading hitters and taking advantage of their flaws.

To maintain your composure: Although pressure is unavoidable, you must not allow it to distort your judgment. Concentrate on the task at hand, take some deep breaths, and have faith in the preparation you've made. There is a correlation between being rattled, making predictable pitches, and missing opportunities.

Recurring errors from the past should not be a source of distraction. With each new pitch comes a fresh opportunity. Adjust your strategy, learn from what did not work, and concentrate on the next pitch.

You may change from a reactive pitcher into a proactive one by combining rigorous observation, strategic pitch selection, and unshakable mental focus. This will allow you to become an expert at reading hitters and taking advantage of their weaknesses. It is important to remember that the top pitchers are not simply throwers but also strategists who can take advantage of their opponents and control the game's flow.

Handling pressure

"In high-stakes situations."

Imagine that there are two outs, the bases are loaded, and it is the bottom of the ninth. A thunderous roar is coming from the crowd, and the tension is so thick that it could be sliced with a knife. As the pitcher, you are the focus of everyone's attention because the game's outcome is in your hands. Your mental fortitude, in addition to your physical abilities, will be put to the test in this predicament, which is the pinnacle of high-stakes situations. How can you remain calm under pressure and perform best when it means the most?

To achieve success, it is essential to develop mental resilience

Contemplate a structure; to survive any storm, it is necessary to have a solid foundation. Like physical resilience, mental resilience is the foundation for successfully managing pressure in high-pressure situations. To cultivate these vital traits, here are some:

- ◆ **Confidence:** Have faith in your capabilities and the effort that you have put in. You can boost your confidence in your abilities by visualizing yourself achieving and concentrating on your previous achievements.

♦ Tune out the noise and distractions so that you can concentrate. Bring your attention to the work at hand, the next pitch, or the next play, and narrow your focus. Remain present now and avoid dwelling on the outcome of the expectations set.

♦ Keep a cheerful attitude even when things don't go as planned, even if negative things happen. A pessimistic outlook can snowball, resulting in decreased performance and more self-doubt. Focus on the things you control and learn from your failures.

Tools for the Toolbox: Developing Effective Coping Mechanisms for Overcoming Stress

Imagine you have a toolbox full of different tools you can use in various scenarios. Identify and cultivate a variety of coping techniques to efficiently manage pressure:

♦ It would help to practice deep breathing to calm your anxieties and slow your pulse rate. Take slow, deep breaths. This benefits of regaining your focus and regulating your physiological stress response.

♦ Replacing negative thoughts with positive affirmations is known as positive self-talk. Bring to mind your accomplishments and the qualities that make you unique.

♦ **Visualization:** Before walking onto the mound, visualize yourself executing pitches beautifully and navigating the pressure with poise. Because of this mental repetition, confidence is increased, and favorable outcomes are reinforced.

- ◆ The establishment of pregame routines that offer a sense of comfort and familiarity is an important aspect of the game.
- ◆ Examples include specialized stretches, activities involving visualization, or listening to calming music.

Converting Anxiety into Fuel: Accepting the Pressure with Gratitude

Consider a car's engine; it can go forward with power if given the appropriate fuel quantity. When properly managed, pressure has the potential to be an extremely effective motivator.

Channel the Energy: Make the most of the rush of adrenaline that you are experiencing. You must transform your nervous energy into concentrated intensity to perform at your highest level.

The Challenge Is Yours to Accept: Take the opportunity to demonstrate your abilities and rise to the situation by viewing pressure as an opportunity. This change in perspective has the potential to transform worry into enthusiasm and a desire to achieve success.

One Pitch at a Time: Maintaining a Present Attitude

Imagine a lengthy trip: it can be nerve-wracking to concentrate on the goal at the end of the journey. Reduce the amount of pressure to a more tolerable level.

Pay Attention to the Procedure: Do not become preoccupied with the game's result. The most important thing is to execute each pitch precisely, one at a time. Rely on the procedure, and let your abilities take the lead.

Recurring errors from the past should not be a source of distraction: Gain knowledge from them, adjust your strategy, and concentrate on the next pitch. Every pitch presents a fresh opportunity to achieve success.

Being able to handle pressure in high-stakes circumstances is a skill that may be cultivated via practice and awareness of oneself during the process. You may turn yourself from a player overwhelmed by the occasion to a performer who thrives under the spotlight by cultivating mental resilience, creating coping methods, and accepting your strain.

CHAPTER 3

FIELDING YOUR POSITION

Covering bunts and making plays

Now, picture a situation where a runner is on first base, the batter squares around, and the crowd goes completely silent. It is time to execute a bunt, a tactical maneuver that has the potential to alter the way a game is played. As a fielder, you must have anticipation, quick reflexes, and good communication to cover bunts and make plays. A rundown of the most critical aspects is as follows:

Understanding the Circumstances: Looking Forward to the Bunt

Not every hitter can be bunted. There are, however, circumstances that increase the likelihood of a bunt:

- **Runners on Base:** When runners are on base, a bunt can help advance the lead runner and pressure the defense.
- When the score is tied or close, a bunt can be a calculated gamble to score a run in a very close game.
- A hitter having difficulty hitting may turn to bunt to get to base if they are having difficulty hitting.

You can improve your chances of predicting a bunt by first gaining an awareness of these conditions and then observing the body language of the hitter.

Bunt Defenses: When it comes to winning, teamwork is the key

Bunt defenses can take various forms, depending on the base circumstances and the coach's approach. The following are some widespread examples:

No Outs: When there are no outs, the main objective of the defense is to get the batter out of the game. The infielders make a determined effort to cover the bunt, with the pitcher protecting first base, the second baseman covering second base, and the third baseman covering home base.

Runners on First and Second: The "Wheel Play" is frequently utilized to accomplish this scenario. First basemen are responsible for charging the bunt, second basemen are the ones to cover first, and shortstops are the ones to cover second. If the ball is fielded, the pitcher will cover third base, while the third baseman will remain in the outfield and cover home.

Runner on First Only: In this scenario, the first baseman is the one who charges the bunt, the second baseman is the one who covers initially, and the shortstop is the one who covers later. If the ball is fielded, the pitcher will cover third base, while the third baseman will remain behind to cover home.

It is essential to communicate: As the player with the best perspective of the field, the catcher typically instructs the defense by calling out the play based on the direction the bunt is facing.

Putting the Bunt in the Field: Taking Charge

Rapid action is necessary once a bunt has been established. A variety of players respond to the circumstance in the following ways:

- The pitcher charges the ball bunted, intending to field it cleanly and produce a rapid throw to first base.
- If the ball is ruled foul, the first baseman will charge the bunt and be prepared to either field it or backpedal to cover first base.
- If the first baseman charges, the second baseman will cover first base. If the bunt is headed toward the outfield, the second baseman will cover second base.
- The third baseman is responsible for either charging toward the bunt or staying back to cover home plate, depending on the defenses in place.

Consider that to field a bunt properly; you need quick reactions, solid footwork, and a strong throw.

Putting the Piece Together: Transforming Defense into Offence

When the bunt is successfully fielded, the attention changes to making an out. Here are some important things to keep in mind:

When it comes to throwing mechanics, it is essential to make a powerful and accurate throw to the intended base while maintaining a tight hold on the ball.

Base Coverage: Communicate with your teammates to ensure every aspect of the game is looked after. The catcher may request a throw to first, second, or third base, depending on the circumstances.

If feasible, you should strive to get a force out at a base that a runner already occupies. A bunt defense can transform a potential offensive threat into a defensive advantage.

When it comes to honing your skills, practice makes perfect

Continuous training is necessary to cover bunts and make plays efficiently. Drills such as:

- Working on footwork and throwing mechanics
- Simulating bunt situations with teammates
- Fielding bunts hit at varying speeds and directions
- Working on bunt situations while playing with teams

Your ability to respond quickly and execute effectively can be considerably improved.

You can develop into a self-assured and dependable fielder who is prepared to deal with every bunt situation that may come along, provided that you have a thorough awareness of the various bunt defenses, that you anticipate the play, and that you practice the necessary abilities. Remember that a good defense may be the driving force behind a successful team, and efficiently covering bunts is essential.

Working with infielders

"On double plays."

To accomplish the task of turning a single play into a double play, a symphony of coordinated movement and flawless execution must take place. It is crucial to thoroughly understand the key components and drills necessary to produce seamless and successful double-play turns while working with infielders, whether as a coach or a player. This is true whether you are working with infielders voluntarily or as a coach.

Obtaining an Understanding of the Multiplicity of Double Plays

It is the most common sort of double play, and it consists of a ground ball to the second baseman, who then throws to the shortstop for a force out at second and then throws to first for the second out. Turn Two is the most common type of double play. Turn Four is a play that is used less frequently and consists of a ground ball to the first baseman, who then throws to the second baseman for a force out at second base and then a throw to shortstop for the second out. This play is referred to as the "turn four. "A double-play ball is a ball that is hit inside the range of the infielders and opens the door for a potential double-play opportunity. This type of ball is referred to as a double-play ball.

What is most important is communication.

The obligation of calling the play and delivering the ball to the appropriate base ultimately falls on the shoulders of the second baseman, depending on the situation's specifics. It is essential to communicate clearly and concisely to reduce the amount of uncertainty that occurs and the number of missed opportunities.

Verbal cues include the following: Since it is essential to guarantee that all individuals are on the same page, the shortstop and the first baseman verbally confirm the call. The mechanics of the foot and throwing techniques are as follows:

- The second baseman must acquire a quick first step and efficient footwork when playing the position to reach the ball and perform a forceful and accurate throw to the shortstop (also known as the shortstop).

- It is essential to practice receiving throws while sprinting and pivoting to throw to first base when playing shortstop. This is because it is necessary to throw to first base.

- The responsibility for this lies with the first baseman, who must position himself strategically and react swiftly to catch the throw from the shortstop for the final out.

To improve One's Capabilities: The drills.

When practicing ground ball drills, it is essential to simulate various double-play scenarios by hitting them to different infield portions. This will help you get the most out of your practice sessions. During the process of learning double play turns, it is essential to practice the entire cycle of fielding, throwing, and receiving the ball for each variation of the double play.

Practices for Footwork: One of the essential things that every infielder taking part in the play should concentrate on is improving their agility and taking quick first steps.

The Accuracy of Throwing: The performance of throws that are accurate and consistent with the target base should be greatly emphasized.

Getting oneself mentally ready to go

The score, the number of runners on base, and the type of hitter are all factors infielders should consider when attempting to predict the likelihood of double plays occurring. Maintain concentration throughout the play by avoiding distractions and carrying out each step with uncompromising accuracy throughout the performance.

When it comes to the construction of a powerful infield unit

Frequent practice sessions must be dedicated to double-play drills to establish muscle memory and ensure seamless execution under pressure. This can be accomplished by practicing regularly. Providing positive reinforcement to the infield players is essential to foster a sense of team spirit and confidence. This can be achieved by encouraging positive communication and celebrating successful double plays.

Among the Most Cutting-edge Methods:

If the batter is at second base, the second baseman has the option of either forcing the batter out or allowing the batter to tag out. This decision is made based on the specific circumstances of the situation. Even though it is a more sensible choice, a force-out requires flawless footwork to guarantee that the runner is not in danger. The usage of a tag out is an option for those who desire greater freedom; however, it is necessary to have a quick tag. In the context of double-play depth, infielders adjust their location following the situation at the base. To reduce the gap between them and speed up the play, they move closer to the base when there are runners on base. This allows them to move more quickly.

Having an Awareness of the Circumstances

But Defense: When the infielders anticipate a bunt, they may shift their positions to prioritize getting the lead runner out of the game. This is done to prevent the bunt from being successful.

Errors in Fielding: If a fielding error occurs when the team attempts to double-play, the infielders must adjust and respond quickly to salvage the situation.

Establishing Chemistry: Trust and communication are the cornerstones upon which a strong infield unit is constructed through the establishment of chemistry. Through the utilization of positive reinforcement and the implementation of frequent teambuilding activities, it is possible to nurture the development of a sense of camaraderie and shared responsibility among participants. As part of the preparation for game day, having a chat about potential double-play scenarios that are specific to the upcoming opponent and reviewing scouting reports are both things that are included in the process.

Double plays are a typical occurrence in situations involving a lot of pressure, so mental toughness is essential. It is of the utmost importance that infielders maintain their composure, focus their attention specifically on the task at hand, and do not allow missed opportunities to harm their overall performance.

To become an expert in converting double plays, it is necessary to have dedication, practice consistently, and employ a methodical plan that focuses on communication, footwork, throwing accuracy, and mental fortitude. You can change your defense into a formidable opponent by implementing these strategies and cultivating a strong sense of team spirit within the infield. This defense can turn the tide of any game with a double play that is executed perfectly, and it can do so by implementing these strategies.

Proper techniques

"For backing up bases"

Imagine that a play has been done flawlessly, and the ball is flying through the air, but a vital component is missing adequate backup. Regarding a strong defense, backing up bases is the unseen guardian that ensures a safety net for throws that can go astray and prevent the opponent from gaining more bases. The following is a rundown of the appropriate methods available for backing up bases:

Realizing Your Place in the Game

The following are the backup responsibilities that are assigned to each player based on their position:

- In the event of a wayward throw or an erroneous attempt to pick off the base, the first baseman is responsible for covering the base and backing up throws to first base.
- It is the responsibility of the second baseman to provide backup for throws to the second base and to cover the base for any potential overthrows from the shortstop or throws from the outfield.

- While covering the base for throws from the outfield or probable overthrows from the third baseman, the shortstop is responsible for providing backup for throws to the shortstop position.
- The third baseman is responsible for providing backup for throws to the third base and covering the base before any potential overthrows from the shortstop or throws from the outfield.
- The outfielders are responsible for making backup throws to their respective bases, offering a safety net, and preventing runners from making further progress.

Finding the Right Position

It is important for players to position themselves strategically according to the available circumstances:

- Because backup positions are closer to the base while runners are on base, they can react more quickly and throw the ball further.
- The backup positions can be moved further back when there are no runners on base, which provides a greater range of coverage.

One of the Most Important Things:

To prevent collisions and ensure everyone is aware of their responsibilities, fielders need to communicate clearly with one another. "Ball!" should be yelled out by the fielder who is receiving the throw to alert the player in the backup. Backup players must acknowledge the call and respond appropriately by adjusting their positioning.

Playing the Field and Footwork

The ability to make quick changes and field erroneous throws effectively is made possible by having proper footwork:

♦ Keep your knees slightly bent and maintain a balanced posture while preparing to react fast.

♦ You can use fast shuffles or short steps to make any necessary adjustments to your position.

♦ You should be ready to field the ball in a tidy manner, and if necessary, you should use a twohanded approach.

For Honing Skills: Drills

Drills for backing up involve simulating various situations in which throws could go wrong, and players practice backing up their bases allotted to them. Implementing verbal signals into backing up drills and emphasizing unambiguous calls and acknowledgment is an important part of communication drills. Within the context of backing-up drills, fielding drills should include fielding erroneous throws to train with unexpected scenarios.

The focus of the Mind

Anticipation: Maintain vigilance and anticipate probable throws that might call for support.

Maintaining focus throughout the play: even when you are not directly involved, you can respond quickly if required.

Putting Together a Powerful Defense

Regular Practice: It is essential to have regular practice sessions that are dedicated to backing up drills to create muscle memory and provide smooth reactions throughout the training process. Fostering a sense of duty and a sense of team spirit within the defense can be accomplished through positive reinforcement, which includes encouraging constructive communication and celebrating successful backups.

Consciousness of the Situation

Having an understanding of the game is essential, as the methods of backing up can change depending on the circumstances:

- When runners are on base, backup positions are moved closer to the base to prevent extra base advances. This is done to avoid outs. Positions can be moved significantly further back when outs are used to provide wider coverage.

- Backup positions may shift when balls are hit to particular places to anticipate probable throws. This is referred to as the hit location. Taking a ground ball to the right side as an example, outfielders backing up third base on the ground ball.

- If the defense becomes shifted, the backup positions must be adjusted correspondingly to fill the voids generated by the shift.

Methods of the Highest Order

Players Who Are Considered to Be Cutoffs: Certain players may be recognized as cutoffs within certain circumstances. The players in this, position themselves strategically to intercept erroneous throws and prevent additional bases from being scored.

Rundowns: Backup players are extremely important during rundowns since they are responsible for keeping the runner from making any progress. If they want to stop the runner, they need to be aware of the situation and anticipate any throws that could be made.

Not Just the Fundamentals

- The importance of hustle: Despite the fact that the throw may appear ordinary, you should always rush towards your backup position. Even a fraction of a second can make a difference when preventing an additional base.
- You should always be ready for anything, even the most improbable tosses. A heads-up play may save the day.
- Each player on the pitch is accountable for providing support to the base they have been allocated. A sense of accountability is fostered within the team when members take ownership of their work.

When it comes to a successful defense, one of the unsung heroes is frequently the appropriate backing-up strategies. You can transform your team into a defensive force by first gaining a grasp of your function, then positioning yourself tactically, then speaking properly, then practicing diligently, and finally keeping a focused and attentive attitude. This will allow you to be ready to shut down the enemy and prevent costly blunders. It is important to make every out, and a backup that is handled successfully can be the difference between a close play and a circumstance that completely changes the game. It is important to remember that solid backing up is the glue that keeps a strong defense together, so ensure you do not underestimate its potency.

CHAPTER 4

THE MENTAL GAME

Developing focus and resilience.

Just for a moment, try to picture yourself walking a tightrope as the wind rages around you, attempting to distract you. This is how life might feel at times, requiring us to maintain our concentration and resiliency to handle the obstacles that come our way successfully. These two characteristics are not merely mental states but talents that can be developed by deliberate effort and consistent practice. There are a few ways in which you might cultivate attention and resilience:

Working to Improve Your Focus

Identifying Distractions: Recognize what causes your attention to be diverted from the work currently being performed. Environmental noises, internal concerns, and social media could all be contributing factors.

Minimize distractions by turning off notifications, clearing up clutter from your workspace, and selecting a quiet workplace. This will help you create an environment that is conducive to concentration.

Mindfulness Techniques: Mindfulness activities, such as meditation or deep breathing, can help you train your mind to be present and focused. The process of setting clear goals involves defining distinct and attainable goals for each work. In addition to assisting in maintaining your motivation, this offers a particular path for your concentration.

To break down tasks, huge projects should be broken down into smaller, more manageable segments. Because of this, they become less daunting, and you can concentrate on taking one step at a time.

To build resilience

The belief that difficulties are chances for learning and development is an essential component of developing a growth mindset. This enables you to recover quickly from failures and keep a positive attitude throughout the process. One way to find meaning in challenges is to look at them as steppingstones toward achieving a more significant objective. Adding this gives your problems a purpose, which strengthens your resolve to triumph over them. As part of constructing a support system, it is important to surround yourself with positive and supporting folks who will encourage you and provide assistance when challenges arise. As part of your self-care routine, make it a priority to engage in activities that benefit your mind, body, and spirit. Exercising, eating healthily, getting sufficient sleep, and engaging in activities you enjoy are all examples of this. Learn from your mistakes by analyzing your failures and determining the areas in which you can make improvements. This enables you to approach future challenges with a significantly more informed perspective. Irrespective of how insignificant your accomplishments may seem; it is important to recognize and honor them. You will feel more confident as a result of this, as it will reinforce your sense of accomplishment.

Collaboratively Developing Concentration and Resilience

Focus Improves Resilience: Concentration Keeping your attention throughout the process enables you to confront problems head-on, increasing your potential to prevail over them.

Resilience helps to strengthen focus, as follows: Having the knowledge that you can recover from failures enables you to keep your concentration even when you are confronted with distractions or challenges.

Self-Compassion and Mindfulness: an Introduction Self-compassion and mindfulness activities benefit both the ability to concentrate and remain resilient. You can better manage stress, create a positive inner voice, and maneuver through problems with greater ease if you possess these abilities.

The process of cultivating focus and resilience is ongoing. On certain days, distractions will prevail, and difficulties will appear insurmountable. However, you may acquire these vital talents by constantly practicing the tactics discussed above. This will enable you to handle life's problems with greater clarity, resolve, and a sense of purpose. You will be able to maintain your concentration on your objectives, even when the wind is blowing violently, and you will emerge from every challenge you face more powerful and more resilient than before.

Strategies for maintaining composure.

Consider the following situations in which it may feel like an uphill battle to maintain composure: a heated debate, an impending deadline, or a public performance. Each of these scenarios is an example of a situation where it may feel like you are fighting an uphill battle. The ability to keep one's cool and remain composed in the face of adversity is a skill that is valuable in every aspect of life, even though this is the case. The following are some strategies that will help you maintain your composure in the face of certain situations:

Immediately, at this exact instant

Inhale deeply and slowly for a few moments. By doing this simple step, you will be able to reduce the rate at which your heart beats and calm your nervous system, which will ultimately enable you to think more clearly.

Before responding to the situation, I would appreciate it if you could take a moment to pause and think about it. Because of this, you will have the opportunity to collect your thoughts and assess the situation. Because of this, you are prevented from making hasty choices that could cause you to realize your regret.

Confront Your Thoughts and Ideas: Are you exacerbating the problem much more than it is? To make your unpleasant thoughts more bearable and grounded in reality, you need to transform them into different opinions.

Be sure to engage in constructive self-talk: When you want to boost your self-confidence and resilience, it is helpful to remind yourself of the things you have accomplished in the past and your qualities.

Some of the physical tactics are as follows.

- To decrease tension and promote relaxation, you can perform a technique known as progressive muscle relaxation. This technique involves tensing and releasing different muscle groups located throughout your body.

- By engaging in mindfulness exercises, you can help yourself become more rooted in the here and now and reduce the emotional reaction you experience. Concentrating on your breath or the sensations occurring in your body is the emphasis of these exercises.

- One can improve their ability to manage stress and boost their capacity to regulate emotions by engaging in regular physical activity.

The Long-term Strategies for the Organization

It is recommended that you adopt a growth mindset, which means that you should not perceive challenges as failures but rather as opportunities for learning and development inside. It is important to treat oneself with the same level of kindness that you would show to a close friend. This means noticing your emotions without passing judgment on them. Self-compassion is the discipline that comes from this. It would help if you surrounded yourself with people who are positive and supportive and who can offer you encouragement and direction while you are going through difficult situations. This will allow you to establish a support system for yourself. You must give your health and well-being a high priority. It is vital to receive an adequate amount of sleep, consume nutritious foods, and participate in activities that you enjoy to maintain mental and emotional equilibrium. This can be accomplished by engaging in activities that you enjoy.

Among the additional useful hints are

Recognize the situations or people that tend to kick off your intense reactions and give them the attention they deserve. Because of this understanding, you can anticipate and ensure that you are prepared for any potential challenges that may come up. One of the components of developing coping mechanisms is Utilizing stress management techniques that are helpful to your health, such as maintaining a journal, listening to music, or spending time in nature. These are all examples of stress management techniques. Imagining oneself effectively navigating stressful situations is an example of the discipline known as visualization. This mental practice may strengthen both one's sense of self-assurance and one's ability to control their emotions. Suppose you find it difficult to maintain your composure on your own. In that case, you might want to consider going to therapy or counseling to develop skills for coping with stressful situations and address the issues at the root of the problem.

> *One's capacity to maintain composure is a skill that may be improved by consistent practice and a heightened knowledge of one's capabilities. There are going to be times when you fall short of your goals, and that is wholly fine. Building up your emotional resilience over time, putting these strategies into action, and gaining knowledge from your experiences are the most significant things you can do to improve your emotional resilience. If you regularly put in the effort, you can develop the talent of negotiating the challenges that life throws at you with greater tranquility, clarity, and confidence in your ability to govern yourself.*

The role of a pitcher as a team leader

Even though baseball is frequently regarded as a sport played by individuals in isolated positions, the duty of a pitcher encompasses a great deal more than simply throwing strikes. A successful pitcher exemplifies the attributes of a genuine team leader since they can influence the momentum of the game as well as the morale of their teammates. To better understand the numerous factors that define the leadership position of a pitcher, below is a breakdown:

Creating an Atmosphere

Composure and control: A pitcher is responsible for establishing the mood for the entirety of the game. They have a tremendous impact on the enthusiasm and attention of the team because of their ability to maintain composure under duress, their ability to regulate the speed of play, and their overall demeanor.

An Attitude of Competitiveness: The competitive attitude is infectious and spreads quickly. Pitchers who exhibit an unyielding passion to win and compete at the greatest level motivate their teammates to push themselves beyond their personal and professional boundaries.

Taking Charge Through Effective Communication

Working in conjunction with the Catcher: One of the most critical components of a team's defense is the pitcher-catcher battery. They must communicate effectively with one another to achieve success in terms of pitch selection, defensive positioning, and overall strategy.

Encouragement and inspiration are provided by the following: The best leaders are those who inspire their followers. Pitchers can maintain A favorable environment in the dugout by offering encouragement after a problematic play, celebrating defensive triumphs, and maintaining a positive vibe.

Taking the Lead by Example

The importance of work ethics and preparation: The level of commitment and preparation required of pitchers is the standard. As a result of their dedication to training, researching hitters, and continuously improving their skills, their colleagues are inspired to strive for perfection in their respective roles.

The Importance of Overcoming Obstacles: The pressure and setbacks pitchers encounter are common. Their ability to persevere in the face of hardship, recover quickly from errors, and keep their concentration under challenging circumstances serves as a tremendous example for the entire team.

Past the Mound, we have

A mentality of being a team player: The team's success is more critical to a true leader than the glory of the individual. A strong sense of unity is fostered by pitchers who take the time to recognize and honor the accomplishments of their teammates, make an excellent contribution to the culture of the team, and encourage their fellow players.

Mentorship and guidance are provided by: More seasoned pitchers can serve as mentors to younger players, imparting their expertise, experience, and insights to them to assist them in developing their abilities and boosting their self-assurance.

Leadership is not a term that is conferred upon a player: It is something that is earned by actions and behaviors. Pitchers who exhibit these characteristics have the potential to become the heart and soul of their team, motivating their colleagues to play with passion, determination, and a common goal of achieving victory.

Body Language: The body language of a pitcher conveys a great deal of information. People who project leadership instill confidence in their teammates by adopting a confident posture, maintaining eye contact, and making positive gestures.

"Humility and Accountability:" Acknowledging errors and accepting responsibility for failures demonstrates maturity and humility, which are attributes that resonate with teammates and help establish trust.

Rejoicing in Our Successes: When teammates can experience the joy of success together through shared celebrations, it helps to reaffirm the collective effort and deepens the link between these individuals.

Pitchers can turn themselves from just good athletes into genuine leaders by embracing these leadership traits. This will allow them to leave an indelible mark on their team and the game itself.

CHAPTER 5

TRAINING AND CONDITIONING

Offseason and in-season

"Training routines"

To achieve optimal effectiveness as a pitcher, it is essential to have a well-structured training plan that is followed throughout the year. To maximize their potential, pitchers train in the following manner during the offseason as well as during the existing season:

During the offseason, we start laying the groundwork.

During the offseason, pitchers have the best opportunity to construct a solid foundation of physical traits necessary for competitive success. Because of this period, it is possible to train more frequently without having to worry about the obligations of a regular season schedule:

Strength Training: Develop a strong core and lower body to generate velocity and retain control. This is an essential component of strength training. The foundation of a strength training program is comprised of exercises such as squats, deadlifts, lunges, and core resistance exercises.

Throwing Program: It is essential to have a gradual throwing program to improve arm strength and mechanics. During the offseason, it is customary to begin with light throws and then gradually proceed to simulated game scenarios as training continues. Pitchers can preserve their stamina during the lengthy season by conditioning themselves and building their cardiovascular endurance through running, swimming, or cycling.

Flexibility and Mobility: Keeping the body in proper flexibility and mobility throughout the body helps prevent injuries and enhances throwing mechanics.

It is important to remember that the offseason program should be adapted to each pitcher's specific requirements and objectives. For optimal results, it is strongly recommended to seek the advice of a trained strength and conditioning coach.

During the Season: Keeping Your Performance at Its Peak

During the season, the emphasis switches to ensuring that peak performance is maintained while simultaneously meeting the requirements of a consistent game schedule. In this way, training can be adapted:

Throwing Routine: Compared to the offseason, the intensity of throwing is typically lower, with the primary focus being on preserving mechanics and pitch sharpness through bullpen sessions and game preparation.

Strength Training: Lighter weight training sessions are employed to maintain strength without creating tiredness. Conditioning: High-intensity interval training (HIIT) and plyometrics are frequently utilized to preserve explosiveness and agility.

Recovery and Injury Prevention: Certain activities, such as massage, foam rolling, and getting enough sleep, are essential for preventing injuries and improving muscle recovery.

Most of the time, the team's strength and conditioning coach is responsible for designing in-season training programs. These programs are then modified based on the workload and performance of the pitcher throughout the season.

Things to Take into Account

- **Nutrition:** For the best performance and recovery, it is vital to have a balanced diet abundant in protein, carbs, and good fats. This is true both during the offseason and during the season.
- Pitchers can benefit from mental training by practicing techniques such as mental rehearsal and visualization exercises, which can help them remain focused and keep their composure during games.
- **Sleep:** Making enough sleep a priority is essential for the individual's physical and mental rehabilitation.

Consistency is essential. Pitchers can develop a solid foundation, reach their best throughout the season, and reduce the likelihood of injuries if they adhere to a well-structured training program. Pitchers can maximize their potential and make a substantial contribution to the success of their team if they place equal importance on their mental and physical well-being.

Injury prevention and recovery

Pitchers experience a significant amount of stress on their arms and shoulders due to the constant action of throwing, which is why injury prevention and recovery are essential components of their training procedure. A description of the most important tactics to reduce the likelihood of damage and maximize the likelihood of healing is presented here.

Building a solid foundation is an important part of prevention.

The avoidance of injuries among pitchers is dependent on the use of correct mechanics. Keeping the foot in the proper position, maintaining the ideal arm angle, and following through are all ways to distribute tension uniformly and reduce strain on the arm. In addition, developing a strong core, lower body, and posterior chain muscles helps establish a firm foundation for the throwing motion, which minimizes the likelihood of overuse injuries. Flexibility and mobility are equally crucial to ensuring a smooth throwing action and reducing the possibility of muscular imbalances and strains. This is especially true in the shoulders, elbows, and wrists. To prepare the muscles and facilitate recovery, it is important to prioritize a comprehensive dynamic warmup before throwing and some static stretches afterward. Especially for younger pitchers, adhering to the suggested pitch count recommendations is an effective way to prevent overuse injuries and injuries that could potentially occur.

In conclusion, it is essential to pay attention to your body. Please take note of any pain or discomfort you are experiencing, and do not try to push through it. Allow yourself to rest and, if necessary, seek medical attention.

Recovery is the process of promoting optimal healing.

Recovery and rest are necessary. Muscles and joints can recuperate if there are appropriate rest days between throwing sessions. To alleviate inflammation and swelling, applying ice to places that are painful soon after throwing is helpful. In addition, compression clothing can be beneficial in assisting with the recuperation process. Swimming, cycling, or yoga are light exercises that can help improve blood flow and aid in recovery while reducing the tension placed on the throwing arm. Loosening tight muscles, improving flexibility, and preventing injuries are all benefits that can be gained by regular massage therapy. To treat specific injuries and facilitate appropriate recovery, physical therapy is necessary. It is important to prioritize a nutritious diet because it supplies the body with the resources needed for repair and recovery. These nutrients include protein, carbs, and healthy fats. Maintaining a proper level of hydration is also very important. The body can mend itself and regenerate damaged tissues if it receives adequate sleep.

Other helpful hints include

When it comes to reducing injuries caused by overuse, cross-training is advantageous. Participating in activities that are not related to baseball helps to minimize the repetitive tension that is placed on the pitching arm and exercises different muscle groups. The training of the mind is also essential. Meditation and deep breathing are two relaxation strategies that can help manage stress and increase overall well-being. Stress can make injuries worse. Thus, it is essential to practice these techniques. It is possible to receive individualized guidance on injury prevention, recovery tactics, and appropriate training techniques by consulting a competent sports medicine specialist or athletic trainer.

The prevention of injuries and the rehabilitation from them are continual procedures. Pitchers can reduce the likelihood of suffering injuries, improve their performance, and improve their chances of having a long and successful career on the mound if they give these methods the priority they deserve.

Nutrition and rest

"For peak performance"

The nourishment that athletes put into their bodies and the amount of rest they prioritize are equally as important as the training routine they put into their bodies to achieve optimum performance. Let us look into the power of consuming the appropriate amount of food and enough rest:

What You Should Eat to Fuel Your Body for Optimal Performance

To achieve optimal performance, an athlete's body requires a well-balanced diet rich in carbohydrates, protein, and healthy fats. Carbohydrates are the primary energy source for high-intensity activities like pitching. Consuming whole grains, fruits, and vegetables provides a steady flow of energy. After exercise, protein is crucial for repairing and rebuilding muscle tissue; sources include chicken, fish, beans, and nuts. Healthy fats, found in foods like nuts, seeds, avocados, and olive oil, provide sustained energy, support hormone regulation, and aid nutrient absorption. Vitamins and minerals are also essential for performance, which can be ensured by eating a variety of fruits, vegetables, and whole grains. Proper hydration is critical and consuming a combination of carbs and protein within 30-60 minutes post-exercise helps replenish energy and repair muscles.

Insights about the Power of Rest and Recovery

Adequate sleep (7-9 hours for adults) is crucial for both physical and mental recovery. During sleep, the body repairs muscle tissue strengthens the immune system and improves cognitive function. Listening to your body and prioritizing rest when needed is essential to avoid injuries and maintain performance. Light activities like yoga, swimming, or walking promote active recovery by enhancing blood flow and providing a mental break from intense training. Mental relaxation techniques, such as meditation, deep breathing, and spending time in nature, contribute to overall well-being and can improve sleep and performance.

Utilizing Nutrition and Rest to Their Full Potential for Maximum Performance

Achieving peak performance in baseball requires a comprehensive approach to nutrition and rest. This involves understanding your unique needs and developing a tailored plan to fuel your body and mind optimally. Consult a sports nutritionist to create a personalized nutrition plan based on your goals, training regimen, and body composition. Preparing meals and snacks in advance ensures you have healthy options readily available, saving time and helping you stay on track with your nutrition goals. Consistency in maintaining good nutritional and rest habits is key to sustaining long-term performance. By building a solid foundation of proper nutrition and adequate rest, you'll be able to maintain peak performance throughout your baseball career.

Athletes maximize their physical and mental performance by placing a high priority on proper nutrition and adequate rest. This, in turn, enables them to train more intensely, recover more quickly, and perform at their best on the field. It is important to remember that the food you consume and the amount of sleep you get are not merely supplementary elements; they are crucial instruments for fulfilling your athletic objectives and achieving peak performance.

CHAPTER 6

GAME DAY PREPARATION

Scouting reports

"And strategy planning"

When it comes to gaining an advantage in the complex world of baseball, where every pitch and swing has a significant amount of strategic weight, scouting reports and strategy preparation become indispensable tools. Please allow me to go deeper into the relevance of these two components:

It is said that scouting reports are the "eyes and ears" of the match

Scouting reports are in-depth examinations of players generated by skilled specialists who see them engaging in their respective activities. The physical characteristics, mechanics, pitching arsenal, hitting approach, and strengths and weaknesses of the player are all analyzed in these studies, which provide invaluable insight. A complete review of mechanics, including throwing mechanics for pitchers and hitting mechanics for batters, is also included in the evaluation process. Physical characteristics such as height, weight, build, and athleticism are also considered. The studies investigate the effectiveness of the movements, identifying both areas of strength and those that could use some development. Fastball velocity, secondary pitches, command,

and pitch selection trends are all components evaluated while evaluating a pitcher's throwing repertoire. Similar to how the batter's stance, swing mechanics, tendencies against different pitches, and general plate discipline are described, the hitting approach describes the batter's strategy. The information contained in scouting reports is frequently organized into a variety of tiers, ranging from specific player reports that are extremely thorough to more general studies that cover entire teams or leagues.

When it comes to strategy planning, putting knowledge to use is essential.

Following the completion of scouting reports, coaches and managers are able to build strategic plans for approaching forthcoming games, armed with the insights gained from such studies. The planning of the game and the adaptation of plans to the specific strengths and limitations of the opposing team are both required for this endeavor. The starting pitcher matchup, defensive stance against specific batters, and offensive attempts to expose weaknesses are all decisions that coaches make. Choosing the appropriate pitch sequences for each hitter, taking into account their individual inclinations and strengths, is an essential part of pitching strategy. Alterations are made to defensive posture in accordance with the trends of hitters. At the same time, offensive strategy is responsible for determining the batting order and making use of various sorts of hitters in order to generate opportunities. It is necessary to have a comprehensive understanding of the game, the capabilities of your squad, and the information that can be gained from scouting reports in order to develop an effective strategy.

How Scouting and Strategy Work Together to Create Synergy

The preparation of strategy and the preparation of scouting reports are two sides of the same coin. Scouting is the process of gathering all of the raw data, whereas strategy is the process of analyzing and making use of that data in order to obtain a competitive advantage. Scouting reports are helpful in identifying flaws in the opponent club's pitching staff or batting lineup. These deficiencies can be exploited by the opposing side. The ability to create methods that capitalize on these deficiencies and maximize their scoring opportunities is afforded to coaches as a result of this. Making the Most of Your Strengths: Recognizing the strengths and shortcomings of your team is of the utmost importance. Making the most of your strengths while minimizing your weaknesses is an essential part of strategy planning. This involves developing a game plan that makes the most of the skills of your team. The ability to adapt is essential: No strategy is entirely foolproof. Both scouting reports and strategies need to be flexible enough to be adapted to the current scenario in the game. In order to achieve success, it is essential to analyze how the opposing team is responding and alter your strategy accordingly.

Going Beyond the Fundamentals:

Technology and Analytics: A growing number of scouting and strategy decisions are being made with the assistance of advanced analytics and technology. A more in-depth understanding of player performance may be gained through the use of this information, which includes pitch tracking data, spray charts, and thorough statistical analysis. On the other hand, despite the fact that data and analytics are really useful tools, the human aspect continues to be extremely important. In order to provide significant insights that statistics alone are unable to capture, experienced coaches and scouts are able to assess data and observations with a nuanced understanding of the game.

Scouting reports and strategy planning are continual procedures that require continuous review and adaptation in order to be successful. There is a great opportunity for clubs to acquire a considerable advantage in the ever-changing game of baseball if they make efficient use of these technologies.

Warmup routines

"And pregame rituals"

When it comes to pitchers, the pregame routine is an essential ritual that helps them become psychologically and physically ready for the confrontation that is about to take place on the mound. The body and mind are prepared for optimal performance through the execution of a sequence of warmup exercises and mental preparation that has been meticulously devised. In this section, we will examine the essential elements that constitute a well-structured warmup routine and pregame rituals:

The importance of warmup routines in preparing the body for action

In order to get muscles ready for the demands of throwing, an effective warmup exercise should gradually increase blood flow, raise core temperature, and activate muscles. To get your heart rate up and your blood flowing, you should start with basic cardiovascular exercises. Exercises such as light jogs, jumping jacks, and dynamic stretches are examples of this. It is essential to activate the lower body, which includes performing exercises like as lunges, squats, and leg swings to engage the muscles of the lower body in order to achieve power and stability. After that comes the activation of the upper body, which includes shoulder rolls, arm circles, and mild throws that gradually engage the muscles of the upper body, particularly the arm that is used for throwing. The practice of dynamic stretching helps to enhance flexibility and range of motion, both of which are crucial for preserving correct mechanics and avoiding accidental injuries.

Throwing Progression

Short tosses are the first step in the progression of throwing, which helps to gradually warm up the arm and ensure that good mechanics are being used. Following that, the long toss simulates the tension of the game by increasing the throwing distance while the arm warms up. At last, a bullpen session consists of throwing a certain number of pitches, often between twenty and thirty, with the primary focus being on mechanics and pitch control.

The mental preparation that comes with pregame rituals

The pregame rituals are an essential part of the mental preparation for the game, and they are performed in addition to the physical warmup. It is necessary to engage in visualization because envisioning excellent pitching performances increases both confidence and concentration. When you engage in positive self-talk, you replace negative ideas with affirmations such as "I am focused" or "I trust my abilities." When you listen to motivational music, your energy levels increase, and you develop a more optimistic mentality. Practicing breathing techniques, such as deep breathing, can help to calm nerves and improve concentration. The practice of certain players' superstitions, such as wearing particular garments or performing a fortunate charm, contributes to the players' sense of routine and confidence.

Utilizing an Individualized Approach

There is a great lot of individuality involved in the optimum warmup regimen and pregame rituals. Experimentation is essential to determine what works best for each pitcher. This will ensure that the pitcher is effectively prepared, both physically and psychologically, to perform at their highest level on the mound.

Other helpful hints include:

To guarantee that you perform at your best, make sure that you stay hydrated throughout the warmup and the pregame. Prior to the game, you should avoid eating large meals and instead opt for light snacks that provide prolonged energy. Incorporate your catcher into workouts that involve visualization, acting out different game scenarios, and practicing communication. To ensure that your muscles remain at a comfortable temperature, dress appropriately for the weather. Above all else, have faith in the process, have faith in your talents to stride onto the mound with self-assurance, and believe in the ability to train and prepare.

Pitchers can prepare their bodies and minds for optimal performance by sticking to a well-structured warmup routine and establishing successful pregame rituals. This enables them to take the mound with concentration, self-assurance, and the preparation to dominate the game.

In-game adjustments

"And communication"

There is a constant struggle for modifications and adaptations that take place between the pitcher and the batter in the game of baseball, which is a dynamic dance. When it comes to success, the ability to analyze situations, make adjustments on the fly, and communicate effectively with one's catcher is of the utmost importance for a pitcher. Consider the following as we delve into the complexities of in-game modifications and communication:

Reading the Hitter

Throughout the course of the game, a pitcher will analyze the hitter's stance, swing mechanics, and prior at-bats in order to determine the hitter's particular strengths and weaknesses. This insight facilitates the adjustment of pitch selection. There is a possibility that it will require utilizing different spots within the strike zone or delivering more pitches that are off-speed to a batter who has an excellent knowledge of the fastball. It is essential to throw the batter off balance; therefore, it is necessary to change the speed and position of pitches in order to make it difficult for the batter to anticipate what will be thrown at them.

Modifications Made in the Middle of the Pitch

The sequencing of pitches has a considerable impact on their effectiveness. A pitch sequence that is well-sequenced can either build up a strikeout pitch or force an extremely weak ground ball. Additionally, during the course of an at-bat, batters make modifications to their swing. The ability to recognize these modifications and adjust one's approach accordingly is essential for a competent pitcher. Altering the timing of their delivery or producing a pitch that is different from what was initially planned could be one way to do this.

What is the Most Important Function of Communication?

The catcher occupies a crucial position in the communication process. They offer helpful insights into the tendencies of the hitter, suggestions for pitch selection, and commentary on the mechanics of the pitcher. Their contributions are invaluable. All forms of communication, verbal and nonverbal, are necessary for effective communication. Catchers and pitchers work together to build a common language of signs and signals that allows them to convey pitch selection, location, and strategy without giving the batter additional information. A good relationship between the pitcher and the catcher that is founded on trust is crucial.

In order to adjust to the current game situation

The pressure of the game situation can dramatically impact the psyche of a pitcher. An approach that is calm and focused is required in order to adjust to a situation in which the score is tight, or the bases are loaded. This may necessitate a change in pitch selection or strategy. Baseball is a game that involves swings of momentum. To be successful as a pitcher, one must be able to modify their strategy according on the progression of the game. A string of hits may need a more cautious strategy, whilst a string of strikeouts may call for a more aggressive approach. There is a possibility that both approaches are necessary.

Going Beyond the Fundamentals

The modern game of baseball makes use of in-game analytics to provide real-time data on the effectiveness of pitches, the trends of batters, and ideas for strategic moves. In spite of the fact that it cannot take the place of the pitcher's intuition, this data can be an extremely helpful instrument for making well-informed choices. It is essential to have the capacity to maintain composure and concentration under duress. A skilled pitcher is able to swiftly assess the situation, make necessary adjustments to their strategy, and then go to the next pitch.

The adjustments and communication that take place during the game are an ongoing process that calls for constant analysis, adaptation, and trust between the pitcher and the catcher. Pitchers are able to handle the ever-changing dynamics of the game, keep their cool, and eventually lead their team to victory if they are able to master these qualities.